HOW MANY CHILDREN
HAD LADY MACBETH?

HOW MANY CHILDREN HAD LADY MACBETH?

AN ESSAY IN THE THEORY AND PRACTICE OF SHAKESPEARE CRITICISM

BY

L. C. KNIGHTS

GORDON FRASER
THE MINORITY PRESS, CAMBRIDGE
1933

For P.N.T.

This essay is based upon a paper read before the Shakespeare Association at King's College, London.

HOW MANY CHILDREN
HAD LADY MACBETH?

PART I

§ 1

FOR some years there have been signs of a re-
orientation of Shakespeare criticism. The books
that I have in mind have little in common with
the majority of those that have been written on
Shakespeare, but they are likely to have a
decisive influence upon criticism in the future.
The present, therefore, is a favourable time in
which to take stock of the traditional methods,
and to inquire why so few of the many books
that have been written are relevant to our study
of Shakespeare as a poet. The inquiry involves
an examination of certain critical presuppositions,
and of these the most fruitful of irrelevancies is
the assumption that Shakespeare was pre-
eminently a great "creator of characters." So
extensive was his knowledge of the human
heart (so runs the popular opinion) that he was
able to project himself into the minds of an
infinite variety of men and women and present
them "real as life" before us. Of course, he

was a great poet as well, but the poetry is an added grace which gives to the atmosphere of the plays a touch of "magic" and which provides us with the thrill of single memorable lines and lyric passages.

This assumption that it is the main business of a writer—other than the lyric poet—to create characters is not, of course, confined to criticism of Shakespeare, it long ago invaded criticism of the novel.   I have seen the statement attributed to Mr. Galsworthy that "the novelist who hangs his characters on to his plot, instead of his plot on to his characters is guilty of original sin." "Character creation," says Mr. Logan Pearsall Smith, "is regarded as the very essence of English fiction, the *sine qua non* of novel writing." And in a recent book of extracts from Scott, Mr. Hugh Walpole writes:

> "The test of a character in any novel is that it should have existed before the book that reveals it to us began and should continue after the book is closed. . . .   These are our friends for life—but it is the penalty of the more subconscious school of modern fiction that, when the book is closed, all that we have in our hands is a boot-button, a fragment of tulle, or a cocktail shaker.   We have dived, it seems, so very deep and come to the surface again with so little in our grasp. . . .   But (he continues) however gay, malicious, brilliant and amusing they [modern novels] may be, this hard business of creating a world for us, a world filled with people

in whom we may believe, whom we may know better than we know our friends, is the gift of the very few."[1]

It should be obvious that a criterion for the novel by which we should have to condemn *Wuthering Heights*, *Heart of Darkness*, *Ulysses*, *To the Lighthouse* and the bulk of the work of D. H. Lawrence does not need to be very seriously considered.

There is no need to search for examples in the field of Shakespeare criticism. In the latest book on Shakespeare that has come to hand, we read: "His creations are not *ideas* but *characters* —real men and women, fellow humans with ourselves. We can follow their feelings and thoughts like those of our most intimate acquaintances."[2] The case is even better illustrated by Ellen Terry's recently published *Lectures on Shakespeare*. To her the characters are all flesh and blood and she exercises her ingenuity on such questions as whether Portia or Bellario thought of the famous quibble, and whether it was justified.[3] And how did the Boy in *Henry V* learn to speak French? "Robin's French is

[1] *The Waverley Pageant*, pp. 38–40. Cf. "Here unquestionably Scott has the advantage over us. Character is revealed to him so swiftly that he has very little time to analyse it, in fact the characters come to him rather than he to them."

[2] Ranjee G. Shahani, *Shakespeare Through Eastern Eyes*, p. 177.

[3] *Four Lectures on Shakespeare*, pp. 119–120.

quite fluent. Did he learn to speak the lingo from Prince Hal, or from Falstaff in London, or did he pick it up during his few weeks in France with the army?"[1]   Ellen Terry of course does not represent critical Authority; the point is not that she could write as she did, but that the book was popular. Most of the reviewers were enthusiastic. The *Times Literary Supplement* said that the book showed "the insight of a genius," and the reviewer in the *Times*, speaking of her treatment of Falstaff's page, declared, "To Ellen Terry, Robin was as alive and as real as could be; and we feel as if she had given us a new little friend to laugh with and be sorry for."

And if we wish for higher authority we have only to turn to the essay *On Reading Shakespeare* by Mr. Logan Pearsall Smith which filled most of a recent number of *Life and Letters*.[2]   Mr. Smith, it is not widely enough known, is entitled to respect as the author of *Words and Idioms*, in which he showed the kind of interest in language needed for the critical approach to Shakespeare. But there is nothing of that interest in the present essay. Here Shakespeare is praised because he provides "the illusion of reality," because he puts "living people" upon the stage, because he creates characters who are

[1] *Four Lectures on Shakespeare*, p. 49.
[2] Summer, 1932.

"independent of the work in which they appear
. . . and when the curtain falls they go on
living in our imaginations and remain as real
to us as our familiar friends."—"Those inhabi-
tants of the world of poetry who, in our
imagination, lead their immortal lives apart."[1]

The most illustrious example is, of course,
Dr. Bradley's *Shakespearean Tragedy*. The book
is too well-known to require much descriptive
comment, but it should be observed that the
Notes, in which the detective interest supersedes
the critical, form a logical corollary to the main
portions of the book. In the Lectures on
Macbeth we learn that Macbeth was "exceedingly
ambitious. He must have been so by temper.
The tendency must have been greatly strengthened by his marriage." But " it is difficult
to be sure of his customary demeanour." And
Dr. Bradley seems surprised that "This bold
ambitious man of action has, within certain
limits, the imagination of a poet." These minor
points are symptomatic. It is assumed throughout the book that the most profitable discussion
of Shakespeare's tragedies is in terms of the
characters of which they are composed.—"The
centre of the tragedy may be said with equal

---

[1] Mr. Smith reminds us that, "There are other elements
too in this draught of Shakespeare's brewing—in the
potent wine that came to fill at last the great jewelled cup
of words he fashioned, to drink from which is one of the
most wonderful experiences life affords."

truth to lie in action issuing from character, or in character issuing in action. . . . What we feel strongly, as a tragedy advances to its close, is that the calamities and catastrophe follow inevitably from the deeds of men, and that the main source of these deeds is character. The dictum that, with Shakespeare, 'character is destiny' is no doubt an exaggeration . . . but it is the exaggeration of a vital truth." It is this which leads Dr. Bradley to ask us to imagine Posthumus in the place of Othello, Othello in the place of Posthumus, and to conjecture upon Hamlet's whereabouts at the time of his father's death.

The influence of the assumption is pervasive. Not only are all the books of Shakespeare criticism (with a very few exceptions) based upon it, it invades scholarship (the notes to the indispensable Arden edition may be called in evidence), and in school children are taught to think they have "appreciated" the poet if they are able to talk about the characters—aided no doubt by the neat summaries provided by Mr. Verity which they learn so assiduously before examinations.

In the mass of Shakespeare criticism there is not a hint that "character"—like "plot," "rhythm," "construction" and all our other critical counters—is merely an abstraction from the total response in the mind of the reader or spectator, brought into being by written or spoken words, and that our duty as critics is to examine first the words of which the play is composed, then the total effect which this combination of words produces in our mind. (The two are of course inseparable.) This applies equally to the novel or any other form of art which uses language as its medium. "A Note on Fiction" by Mr. C. H. Rickword in *The Calendar of Modern Letters* expresses the point admirably with regard to the novel: "The form of a novel only exists as a balance of response on the part of the reader. Hence schematic plot is a construction of the reader's that corresponds to an aspect of the response and stands in merely diagrammatic relation to the source. Only as precipitates from the memory are plot or character tangible; yet only in solution have either any emotive valency."[1]

A Shakespeare play is a dramatic poem. It uses action, gesture, formal grouping and symbols, and it relies upon the general conventions governing Elizabethan plays. But, we cannot too often remind ourselves, its end is to

[1] *The Calendar*, October, 1926. In an earlier review, Mr. Rickword wrote, "Mere degree of illusion provides no adequate test: novelists who can do nothing else are able to perform the trick with ease, since 'nothing is easier than to create for oneself the idea of a human being, a figure and a character, from glimpses and anecdotes.' " (*The Calendar*, July, 1926; reprinted in *Towards 'Standards of Criticism,'* Wishart.)

communicate a rich and controlled experience by means of words—words used in a way to which, without some training, we are no longer accustomed to respond. (The general neglect of Hopkins, whose use of words, contrasted, say, with that of Milton or Tennyson, is Shakespearean, shows how far we are from understanding the Shakespearean idiom.) To stress in the conventional way character or plot or any of the other abstractions that can be made, is to impoverish the total response. "It is in the total situation rather than in the wrigglings of individual emotion that the tragedy lies."[1] "We should not look for perfect verisimilitude to life," says Mr. Wilson Knight, "but rather see each play as an expanded metaphor, by means of which the original vision has been projected into forms roughly correspondent with actuality, conforming thereto with greater or less exactitude according to the demands of its nature. . . . The persons, ultimately, are not human at all, but purely symbols of a poetic vision."[2]

It would be easy to demonstrate that this approach is essential even when dealing with plays like *Hamlet* or *Macbeth* which can be made to yield something very impressive in the way of "character." And it is the only approach

[1] M. C. Bradbrook, *Elizabethan Stage Conditions*, p. 102.
[2] G. Wilson Knight, *The Wheel of Fire*, p. 16.

which will enable us to say anything at all relevant about plays like *Measure for Measure* or *Troilus and Cressida* which have consistently baffled the critics. And apart from Shakespeare what are we to say of *Tamburlaine, Edward II, The Revenger's Tragedy* or *The Changeling* if we do not treat them primarily as poems?

Read with attention the plays themselves supply the clue of how they should be read. But those who prefer another kind of evidence have only to consider the contemporary factors which conditioned the making of an Elizabethan play, namely the native tradition of English drama descending from the morality plays, the construction of the playhouse and the conventions depending, in part, upon that construction, and the tastes and expectations of the audience. I have not space to deal with any of these in detail. Schücking has shown how large a part was played in the Elizabethan drama by "primitive technique," but the full force of the morality tradition remains to be investigated. It is, I think, impossible to appreciate *Troilus and Cressida* on the one hand, or the plays of Middleton (and even of Ben Jonson) on the other, without an understanding of the "morality" elements which they contain. As for the second factor, the physical peculiarities of the stage and Elizabethan dramatic conventions, I can only refer to Miss Bradbrook's *Elizabethan Stage*

Conditions. We can make a hasty summary by saying that each of these factors determined that Elizabethan drama should be non-realistic, conditioned by conventions which helped to govern the total response obtained by means of the language of each play. A consideration of Shakespeare's use of language demands a consideration of the reading and listening habits of his audience. Contrary to the accepted view that the majority of these were crude and unlettered, caring only for fighting and foolery, bombast and bawdry, but able to *stand* a great deal of poetry, I think there is evidence (other than the plays themselves) that very many of them had an educated interest in words, a passionate concern for the possibilities of language and the subtleties of poetry. At all events they were trained, by pamphlets, by sermons and by common conversation to listen or to read with an athleticism which we, in the era of the *Daily Mail* and the Best Seller, have consciously to acquire or do our best to acquire. And all of them shared the speech idiom which is the basis of Shakespeare's poetry.[1]

§ 2

We are faced with this conclusion: the only profitable approach to Shakespeare is a

[1] I have presented some of the evidence in an essay on "Education and the Drama in the Age of Shakespeare." *The Criterion,* July, 1932.

consideration of his plays as dramatic poems, of his use of language to obtain a total complex emotional response. Yet the bulk of Shakespeare criticism is concerned with his characters, his heroines, his love of Nature or his "philosophy" —with everything in short, except with the words on the page, which it is the main business of the critic to examine. I wish to consider as briefly as possible how this paradoxical state of affairs arose. To examine the historical development of that kind of criticism which is mainly concerned with "character" is to strengthen the case against it.

A start must be made towards the end of the seventeenth century, and it is tempting to begin with Thomas Rymer. If Rymer is representative his remarks on *Othello*[1] show how completely the Elizabethan tradition had been lost. Of one of the storm speeches (II, i), important both as symbol and ironic commentary, he says, "Once in a man's life, he might be content at *Bedlam* to hear such a rapture. In a Play one should speak like a man of business." He had no conception of the function of rhetoric on the Elizabethan stage; of Othello's speech

O now, for ever
Farewell the Tranquill minde; farewell Content;

he says, "These lines are recited here, not for any thing Poetical in them, besides the sound, that pleases." Combining a demand for realistic

[1] In *A Short View of Tragedy* (1693).

verisimilitude with an acceptance of the neo-
classic canons he has no difficulty in ridiculing
the play:

"The moral, sure, of this Fable is very instructive.

First,   This may be a caution to all Maidens of
Quality how, without their Parents consent, they run
away with Blackamoors.

Secondly,   This may be a warning to all good
Wives that they look well to their Linnen.

Thirdly,   This may be a lesson to Husbands that
before their Jealousie be Tragical the proofs may be
Mathematical."

And so on to the triumphant conclusion:

"What can remain with the Audience to carry
home with them from this sort of Poetry for their
use and edification? how can it work, unless (instead
of settling the mind and purging our passions) to
delude our senses, disorder our thoughts, addle our
brain, pervert our affections, hair our imaginations,
corrupt our appetite, and fill our head with vanity,
confusion, *Tintamarre*, and Jingle-jangle, beyond
what all the Parish Clarks of *London* with their *Old
Testament* farces and interludes, in *Richard* the
second's time, could ever pretend to? . . . The
tragical part is plainly none other than a Bloody
Farce, without salt or savour."[1]

[1] I cannot understand Mr. Eliot's remark that he has
"never seen a cogent refutation of Thomas Rymer's
objections to *Othello*." (*The Sacred Wood*, p. 96.) A
narrow sensibility, a misunderstanding of the nature of
dramatic conventions, and the command of a few debating
tricks (e.g. the description of the play in terms of the
external plot, which would make any tragedy look ridi-
culous) are sufficient to account for his objections. A
point by point refutation is possible but hardly necessary.

But perhaps Rymer is not sufficiently representative for his work to be called as evidence. He had a following which included such critics as Gildon and Dennis, and even Pope was influenced by him, but he was censured by Dryden, Addison and Rowe, amongst others, and the rules he stood for never gained anything like a complete ascendancy in the criticism of the eighteenth century. For evidence of the kind that we require we must turn to Dryden, who was not only "a representative man" but also an enthusiastic admirer of Shakespeare, and if he was not "the father of English criticism," he was at least a critic whose opinions must be reckoned with. When Rymer says of the Temptation scene in *Othello*, "Here we see a known Language does wofully encumber and clog the operation, as either forc'd, or heavy, or trifling, or incoherent, or improper, or most what improbable," it is permissible to disregard him; but when we find that Dryden makes similar remarks of other plays of Shakespeare, it is obvious not only that ways of thought and feeling have changed sufficiently since the Elizabethan period to demand a different idiom, but that the Shakespearean idiom is, for the time being, out of the reach of criticism. In the Preface to his version of *Troilus and Cressida* (1679) Dryden says: "Yet it must be allowed to the present age, that the tongue in general is so much refined since Shakespeare's time that many of his words, and more of his phrases, are scarce intelligible. And of those which we understand, some are ungrammatical, others coarse; and his whole style is so pestered with figurative expressions, that it is as affected as it is obscure." And of *Troilus and Cressida*, "I undertook to remove that heap of rubbish under which many excellent thoughts lay wholly buried . . . I need not say that I have refined the language, which before was obsolete."[1]

Not only the idiom but the Elizabethan conventions were now inaccessible. In the *Defence of the Epilogue* (1672) Dryden takes exception to *The Winter's Tale*, *Love's Labour's Lost* and *Measure for Measure*, "which were either grounded on impossibilities, or at least so meanly written, that the comedy neither moved your mirth, nor the serious part your concernment."

[1] Later he remarks: "I will not say of so great a poet that he distinguished not the blown puffy style from true sublimity; but I may venture to maintain that the fury of his fancy often transported him beyond the bounds of judgment, either in coining of new words and phrases, or racking words which were in use into the violence of a catachresis. It is not that I would explode the use of metaphors from passion, for Longinus thinks 'em necessary to raise it: but to use 'em at every word, to say nothing without a metaphor, a simile, an image, or description, is, I doubt, to smell a little too strongly of the buskin."— The force of Elizabethan language springs from its metaphorical life.

And he proceeds to criticise Fletcher in the true spirit of William Archer.

The implications of Dryden's remarks became the commonplaces of criticism for the succeeding generations. It was permissible to speak of Shakespeare's "Deference paid to the reigning Barbarism" (Theobald), and "The vicious taste of the age" (Hanmer), and to write, "The Audience was generally composed of the meaner sort of people" (Pope), and "The publick was gross and dark. . . . Those to whom our author's labours were exhibited had more skill in pomps or processions than in poetical language" (Johnson). In his *Preface* (1747) Warburton writes,

> "The Poet's hard and unnatural construction . . . was the effect of mistaken Art and Design. The Public Taste was in its Infancy; and delighted (as it always does during that state) in the high and turgid; which leads the writer to disguise a vulgar expression with hard and forced constructions, whereby the sentence frequently becomes cloudy and dark . . . an obscurity that ariseth, not from the licentious use of a single Term, but from the unnatural arrangement of a whole sentence. . . . Not but in his best works (he continues), we must allow, he is often so natural and flowing, so pure and correct, that he is even a model for style and language."

Of all the eighteenth century critics only Johnson (an exception we have often to make) at times transcended the limitations of conventional Shakespeare criticism. He censures Hanmer who in his edition of Shakespeare "is solicitous to reduce to grammar what he could not be sure that his author intended to be grammatical," and he writes admirably of "a style which never becomes obsolete. . . . This style is probably to be sought in the common intercourse of life, among those who speak only to be understood, without ambition of elegance." But he stops short at that. This "conversation above grossness and below refinement, where propriety resides" is where Shakespeare "seems to have gathered his *comick* dialogue." But it is in Shakespeare's tragedies that his style is most vividly idiomatic and full bodied, and Johnson was capable of writing, "His comedy pleases by the thoughts and language, and his tragedy for the greater part by incident and action." Johnson's great virtues as a critic did not include an understanding of Shakespeare's idiom. For him, "The style of Shakespeare was in itself ungrammatical, perplexed and obscure," and many passages remained "obscured by obsolete phraseology, or by the writer's unskilfulness and affectation." We remember also how he could "scarcely check his risibility" at the "blanket of the dark" passage in *Macbeth*.

It should not be necessary to insist that I do

not wish to deny the achievements of the Augustan age in poetry and criticism. But an age of which the commonplaces of criticism were that "Well placing of words, for the sweetness of pronunciation, was not known till Mr. Waller introduced it,"[1] and that Pope's *Homer* "tuned the English tongue";[2] an age which produced the *Essay on Criticism* and the *Satires of Dr. Donne Versified*, and which consistently neglected the Metaphysical poets and the minor Elizabethans, such an age was incapable of fully understanding Shakespeare's use of words. Since the total response to a Shakespeare play can only be obtained by an exact and sensitive study of the quality of the verse, of the rhythm and imagery, of the controlled associations of the words and their emotional and intellectual force, in short by an exact and sensitive study of Shakespeare's handling of language, it is hardly reasonable to expect very much relevant criticism of Shakespeare in the eighteenth century. What can be expected is criticism at one remove from the plays, that is, of every aspect that can be extracted from a play and studied in comparative isolation; of this kind of criticism an examination of "characters" is the most obvious example.

[1] Dryden, *Defence of the Epilogue.*
[2] Johnson, *Life of Pope.*

A significant passage occurs in Shaftesbury's
Advice to an Author, published in 1710:

> "Our old dramatick Poet, Shakespeare, may witness
> for our good Ear and manly Relish.   Notwithstanding
> his natural Rudeness, his unpolish'd style, his anti-
> quated Phrase and Wit, his want of Method and
> Coherence, and his Deficiency in almost all the Graces
> and Ornaments of this kind of Writings; yet by the
> Justness of his *Moral*, the Aptness of many of his
> *Descriptions*, and the plain and natural Turn of
> several of his *Characters*, he pleases his Audience,
> and often gains their Ear, without a single Bribe from
> Luxury or Vice."

We see here the beginning of that process of
splitting up the indivisible unity of a Shakespeare
play into various elements abstracted from the
whole.   If a play of Shakespeare's could not be
appreciated as a whole, it was still possible to
admire and to discuss his moral sentiments, his
humour, his poetic descriptions and the life-
likeness of his characters.   Thus, Warburton
mentions, ". . . the Author's Beauties . . .
whether in Style, Thought, Sentiment, Character,
or Composition."

The intensive study of Shakespeare's characters
was not fully developed until the second half of
the eighteenth century.   Dryden had remarked
that "No man ever drew so many characters, or
generally distinguished 'em from one another,
excepting only Jonson," and Pope observed,

"His *Characters* are so much Nature herself, that 'tis a sort of injury to call them by so distant a name as copies of her. . . . Every single character in Shakespeare is as much an Individual as those in Life itself; it is as impossible to find any two alike"; and Theobald echoed him in a lyrical passage,—"If we look into his Characters, and how they are furnished and proportion'd to the Employment he cuts out for them, how are we taken up with the Mastery of his Portraits! What draughts of Nature! What variety of Originals, and how differing each from the other!"[1] But in the second half of the century character study became one of the main objects of Shakespeare criticism. This is sufficiently indicated by the following titles: *A Philosophical Analysis and Illustration of some of Shakespeare's Remarkable Characters* (Richardson, 1774), *An Essay on the Character of Hamlet* (Pilon, 1777), *Essays on Shakespeare's Dramatic Characters* (Richardson, 1784), *Remarks on some of the Characters of Shakespeare* (Whately, 1785), *Shakespeare's Imitation of Female Characters* (Richardson, 1789), and so on.

Of the essays of this kind, the most famous is Maurice Morgann's *Essay on the Dramatic Character of Sir John Falstaff* (1777). The

---

[1] Pope adds, "Had all the speeches been printed without the very names of the Persons, I believe one might have apply'd them with certainty to every speaker."

pivot of Morgann's method is to be found in
one of his footnotes:

"The reader must be sensible of something in the
composition of *Shakespeare's* characters, which renders
them essentially different from those drawn by other
writers. The characters of every Drama must indeed
be grouped, but in the groupes of other poets the
parts which are not seen do not in fact exist. But
there is a certain roundness and integrity in the
forms of *Shakespeare*, which give them an independence as well as a relation, insomuch that we often
meet with passages which, tho' perfectly felt, cannot
be sufficiently explained in words, without unfolding
the whole character of the speaker. . . . The reader
will not now be surprised if I affirm that those
characters in Shakespeare, which are seen only in
part, are yet capable of being unfolded and understood
in the whole; every part being in fact relative, and
inferring all the rest. It is true that the point of
action or sentiment, which we are most concerned
in, is always held out for our special notice. But
who does not perceive that there is a peculiarity
about it, which conveys a relish of the whole? And
very frequently, when no particular point presses,
he boldly makes a character act and speak from those
parts of the composition which are *inferred* only, and
not distinctly shown. This produces a wonderful
effect; it seems to carry us beyond the poet to nature
itself, and gives an integrity and truth to facts and
character, which they could not otherwise obtain.
And this is in reality that art in *Shakespeare* which,
being withdrawn from our notice, we more emphati-
cally call *nature*. A felt propriety and truth from
causes unseen, I take to be the highest point of

Poetic composition. If the characters of *Shakespeare* are thus *whole*, and as it were original, whilst those of almost all other writers are mere imitation, *it may be fit to consider them rather as Historic than Dramatic beings; and, when occasion requires, to account for their conduct from the* WHOLE *of character, from general principles, from latent motives, and from policies not avowed.*"[1]

It is strange how narrowly Morgann misses the mark. He recognized what can be called the full bodied quality of Shakespeare's work—it came to him as a feeling of "roundness and integrity." But instead of realizing that this quality sprang from Shakespeare's use of words, words which have "a network of tentacular roots, reaching down to the deepest terrors and desires," he referred it to the characters' "independence" of the work in which they appeared, and directed his exploration to "latent motives and policies not avowed." Falstaff's birth, his early life, his association with John of Gaunt, his possible position as head of his family, his military service and his pension are all examined in order to determine the grand question, "Is Falstaff a constitutional coward?"[2]

[1] These last italics are mine.

[2] Falstaff is not a man, but a choric commentary. He is the point at which Shakespeare's attitude towards the action crystallizes. The growth of Shakespeare's dramatic power is seen if we compare his function with that of the Bastard in *King John*. In *King John* the Bastard's speech on Commodity is a single pivotal point. In *Henry IV* the Falstaff attitude is not confined to a single speech but informs the whole play.

In the Essay, of course, "Falstaff is the word only. Shakespeare is the theme," and several admirable things are said incidentally. But more than any other man, it seems to me, Morgann has deflected Shakespeare criticism from the proper objects of attention by his preposterous references to those aspects of a "character" which Shakespeare did not wish to show. He made explicit the assumption on which the other eighteenth century critics based their work, and that assumption has been pervasive until our own time. In 1904 Dr. Bradley said of Morgann's essay, "There is no better piece of Shakespeare criticism in the world."[1]

I have already suggested the main reason for the eighteenth century approach to Shakespeare via the characters, namely an inability to appreciate the Elizabethan idiom and a consequent inability to discuss Shakespeare's plays as poetry. And of course the Elizabethan dramatic tradition was lost, and the eighteenth century critics in general were ignorant of the stage for which Shakespeare wrote.[2] But other factors should also be considered; for instance, the neo-classic insistence upon the moral function of art (before

[1] *The Scottish Historical Review*, Vol. I, p. 291.
[2] "Shakespeare's plays were to be acted in a paltry tavern, to an unlettered audience, just emerging from barbarity."—Mrs. Montagu, *Essay on the Writings and Genius of Shakespeare* (Fifth edition, 1785), p. 13.

you can judge a person in a play he must have more or less human "motives"), and the variations of meaning covered by the term "nature" from the time of Pope to the time of Wordsworth. Literary psychologizing also played a part; Kames and William Richardson[1] both found Shakespeare's persons useful illustrations of psychological theories, and Samuel Richardson fostered an interest in introspective analysis, so that Macbeth's soliloquies were assumed to have something in common with the introspections of Clarissa. Finally (and Richardson serves to remind us) "the sentimental age set in early in the eighteenth century." If we consider any of the Character writers of the seventeenth century, Earle, Overbury or Hall, we find that they preserve a distance from their subjects which the eighteenth century creators of characters do not. The early Characters have a frame round them, whereas the Vicar of Wakefield, Beau Tibbs, and even Sir Roger de Coverley make a more direct appeal to human sympathy and emotion. The "human" appeal ("These are our friends for life . . .") which has made the fortune of Best Sellers, is an intrusion which vitiated, and can only vitiate, Shakespeare criticism.

One form of the charge against eighteenth century Shakespeare criticism is that it made

[1] See Note A.

the approach too easy. In Pope's edition "Some of the most shining passages are distinguish'd by commas in the margin," and Warburton also marked what he considered particularly beautiful passages. From this it was but a step to collect such passages into anthologies. The numerous editions of the collections of *Beauties* show how popular this method of reading Shakespeare had become by the end of the century. This is an obvious method of simplification, but it is only part of the process whereby various partial (and therefore distorted) responses were substituted for the full complex response demanded by a Shakespeare play—a process that was fatal to criticism.[1]

There is no need, even if it were possible, to discuss nineteenth century Shakespeare criticism in detail, partly because it is more familiar, partly because—as Mr. Nichol Smith and Mr. Babcock have helped us to realise—the foundations of modern Shakespeare criticism were laid in the eighteenth century. In the nineteenth century the word "poetry" changed its significance, but preconceptions about "the poetic"

---

[1] A similar fate befell Sterne. See Q. D. Leavis, *Fiction and the Reading Public*, pp. 134–135. For the collections of Shakespeare's *Beauties* I may refer to R. W. Babcock, *The Genesis of Shakespeare Idolatry*, pp. 115–118. The most famous of these anthologies, William Dodd's *Beauties of Shakespeare*, first published in 1752, not only went through many editions in the eighteenth century, but was frequently reprinted in the nineteenth.

derived from reading Keats (or Tennyson) did
not increase understanding of seventeenth century poetry. And everything combined to foster
that kind of interest in Shakespeare which is
represented at certain levels by Mrs. Jameson's
Shakespeare's Heroines and Mary Cowden
Clarke's *Girlhood of Shakespeare's Heroines.* In
so far as the word "romantic" has other than an
emotive use, it serves to distinguish individualist
qualities as opposed to the social qualities
covered by "classical." One of the main results
of the Romantic Revival was the stressing of
"personality" in fiction. At the same time, the
growth of the popular novel, from Sir Walter
Scott and Charlotte Brontë to our own Best
Sellers, encouraged an emotional identification
of the reader with hero or heroine (we all "have
a smack of Hamlet" nowadays).[1] And towards
the end of the century the influence of Ibsen was
responsible for fresh distortions which can best
be studied in *The Old Drama and the New.*

In Shakespeare criticism from Hazlitt to
Dowden we find the same kind of irrelevance.
Hazlitt is capable of writing of Lady Macbeth,

"She is a great bad woman, whom we hate, but
whom we fear more than we hate." And of the

[1] See the letters to popular novelists quoted on p. 58 of
Q. D. Leavis' *Fiction and the Reading Public:* "Your
characters are so human that they live with me as friends,"
etc.

Witches, "They are hags of mischief, obscene panders
to iniquity, malicious from their impotence of enjoyment, enamoured of destruction, because they are
themselves unreal, abortive, half-existences—who
become sublime from their exemption from all
human sympathies and contempt for all human
affairs, as Lady Macbeth does by the force of passion!
Her fault seems to have been an excess of that strong
principle of self-interest and family aggrandisement,
not amenable to the common feelings of compassion
and justice, which is so marked a feature in barbarous
nations and times."

What has this to do with Shakespeare?   And
what the lyric outburst which Dowden quotes
approvingly in his chapter on *Romeo and Juliet?*

"Who does not recall those lovely summer nights,
in which the forces of nature seem eager for development, and constrained to remain in drowsy languor?
. . .   The nightingale sings in the depths of the
woods.   The flower-cups are half-closed."

And so on.

Wherever we look we find the same reluctance
to master the words of the play, the same readi-
ness to abstract a character and treat him (because
he is more manageable that way) as a human
being.   When Gervinus says that the play
Hamlet "transports us to a rude and wild period
from which Hamlet's whole nature recoils, and
to which he falls a sacrifice because by habit,
character and education he is alienated from it,
and like the boundary stone of a changing

civilization touches a world of finer feeling," he exhibits the common fault. In this instance Hamlet is wrenched from his setting and violently imported into the society described by Saxo Grammaticus. Criticism is not all so crass as Sir Herbert Tree's remark that "We must interpret Macbeth, before and at the crisis, by his just and equitable character as a king that history gives him."[1] But there are enough modern instances to show that the advice which Hartley Coleridge gave in *Blackwood's* needed no arguing. "Let us," he said, "for a moment, put Shakespeare out of the question, and consider Hamlet as a real person, a recently deceased acquaintance."[2]

The habit of regarding Shakespeare's persons as "friends for life" or, maybe, "deceased acquaintances," is responsible for most of the vagaries that serve as Shakespeare criticism. It accounts for the artificial simplifications of the editors ("In a play one should speak like a man of business"). It accounts for the "double time" theory for *Othello*. It accounts for Dr. Bradley's Notes and for the criticism in Ward's *History of the English Drama*. It is responsible for all the irrelevant moral and realistic canons which have been applied to Shakespeare's plays, for the sentimentalizing of his heroes (Coleridge

[1] *Illustrated London News*, September 9, 1911.
[2] *Blackwood's Magazine*, Vol. XXIV (1828), p. 585.

and Goethe on Hamlet) and his heroines.   And
the loss is incalculable.   Not only do we lose
the necessary aloofness from a work of art (to
be distinguished from an inability to respond
imaginatively), but we lose the dramatic pattern
and we are inhibited from the full complex
response which a play of Shakespeare's can evoke.
This can only be gained by treating him primarily
as a poet.

PART II

PART II

§ 1

SINCE everyone who has written about Shakespeare probably imagines that he has "treated him primarily as a poet" some explanation is called for. How should we read Shakespeare?

We start with so many lines of verse on a printed page which we read as we should read any other poem. We have to elucidate the meaning (using Dr. Richards' fourfold definition[1]) and to unravel ambiguities; we have to estimate the kind and quality of the imagery and determine the precise degree of evocation of particular figures; we have to allow full weight to each word, exploring its "tentacular roots," and to determine how it controls and is controlled by the rhythmic movement of the passage in which it occurs. In short, we have to decide exactly why the lines "are so and not otherwise."

As we read other factors come into play. The lines have a cumulative effect. "Plot," aspects of "character," recurrent "themes" and "symbols"—all "precipitates from the memory" —help to determine our reaction at a given point.

[1] *Practical Criticism*, pp. 181–183.

There is a constant reference backwards and forwards. But the work of detailed analysis continues to the last line of the last act. If the razor-edge of sensibility is blunted at any point we cannot claim to have read what Shakespeare wrote, however often our eyes may have travelled over the page. A play of Shakespeare's is a precise particular experience, a poem—and precision and particularity are exactly what is lacking in the greater part of Shakespeare criticism, criticism that deals with *Hamlet* or *Othello* in terms of abstractions that have nothing to do with the unique arrangement of words that constitutes these plays.

Obviously what is wanted to reinforce the case against the traditional methods is a detailed examination of a particular play. Unfortunately anything approaching a complete analysis is precluded by the scope of the present essay. The following remarks on one play, *Macbeth*, are, therefore, not offered as a final criticism of the play; they merely point to factors that criticism must take into account if it is to have any degree of relevance, and emphasize the kind of effect that is necessarily overlooked when we discuss a Shakespeare play in terms of characters "copied from life," or of "Shakespeare's knowledge of the human heart."

Even here there is a further reservation to be made. In all elucidation there is an element of crudity and distortion. "The true generalization," Mr. Eliot reminds us, "is not something superposed upon an accumulation of perceptions; the perceptions do not, in a really appreciative mind, accumulate as a mass, but form themselves as a structure; and criticism is the statement in language of this structure; it is a development of sensibility."[1] Of course, the only *full* statement in language of this structure is in the exact words of the poem concerned; but what the critic can do is to aid "the return to the work of art with improved perception and intensified, because more conscious, enjoyment." He can help others to "force the subject to expose itself," he cannot fully expose it in his own criticism. And in so far as he paraphrases or "explains the meaning" he must distort. The main difference between good and bad critics is that the good critic points to something that is actually contained in the work of art, whereas the bad critic points away from the work in question; he introduces extraneous elements into his appreciation—smudges the canvas with his own paint. With this reservation I should like to call the following pages an essay in elucidation.

[1] *The Sacred Wood* (Second edition, 1928), p. 15. See also p. 11 and p. 123, *ibid.*

§ 2

Macbeth is a statement of evil. I use the word "statement" (unsatisfactory as it is) in order to stress those qualities which are "non-dramatic," if drama is defined according to the canons of William Archer or Dr. Bradley. It also happens to be poetry, which means that the apprehension of the whole can only be obtained from a lively attention to the parts, whether they have an immediate bearing on the main action or "illustrate character," or not. Two main themes, which can only be separated for the purpose of analysis, are blended in the play,—the themes of the reversal of values and of unnatural disorder. And closely related to each is a third theme, that of the deceitful appearance, and consequent doubt, uncertainty and confusion. All this is obscured by false assumptions about the category "drama"; *Macbeth* has greater affinity with *The Waste Land* than with *The Doll's House*.[1]

[1] See the Arden edition, p. xxii: "The scenes (Act IV, Scenes II and III) seem to have been composed with evident effort, as if Shakespeare felt the necessity of stretching out his material to the ordinary length of a five-act tragedy, and found lack of *dramatic* material, which was certainly wanting in his authority, Holinshed. *Hence* his introduction in Act V of the famous 'sleep-walking scene' . . . and the magnificently *irrelevant* soliloquies of the great protagonist himself." The italics are mine. There is

Each theme is stated in the first act. The first scene, every word of which will bear the closest scrutiny, strikes one dominant chord:

> Faire is foule, and foule is faire,
> Hover through the fogge and filthie ayre.

It is worth remarking that "Hurley-burley" implies more than "the tumult of sedition or insurrection." Both it and "when the Battaile's lost, and wonne" suggest the kind of metaphysical pitch-and-toss which is about to be played with good and evil. At the same time we hear the undertone of uncertainty: the scene opens with a question, and the second line suggests a region where the elements are disintegrated as they never are in nature; thunder and lightning are disjoined, and offered as alternatives. We should notice also that the scene expresses the same rhythm as the play as a whole: the general crystallizes into the immediate particular ("Where the place?"—"Upon the Heath."—"There to meet with Macbeth.") and then dissolves again into the general presentment of hideous gloom. All is done with the greatest speed, economy and precision.

---

something wrong with a conception of "the dramatic" which leads a critic to speak of Macbeth's final soliloquies as "irrelevant" even though "magnificent." I deal with the dramatic function of Act IV, Scene II and Act IV, Scene III below.

The second scene is full of images of confusion.
It is a general principle in the work of Shakespeare and many of his contemporaries that when
A is made to describe X, a minor character or
event, the description is not merely immediately
applicable to X, it helps to determine the way
in which our whole response shall develop.
This is rather crudely recognised when we say
that certain lines "create the atmosphere" of
the play. Shakespeare's power is seen in the
way in which details of this kind develop, check,
or provide a commentary upon the main interests
which he has aroused.[1]   In the present scene
the description

> Doubtfull it stood,
> As two spent Swimmers, that doe cling together,
> And choake their Art

applies not only to the battle but to the ambiguity
of Macbeth's future fortunes. The impression
conveyed is not only one of violence but of
unnatural violence ("to bathe in reeking wounds")
and of a kind of nightmare gigantism—

> Where the Norweyan Banners flowt the Skie,
> And fanne our people cold.

[1] Cf. Coleridge, *Lectures on Shakespeare, etc.* (Bohn
edition), p. 406: "Massinger is like a Flemish painter, in
whose delineations objects appear as they do in nature,
have the same force and truth, and produce the same
effect upon the spectator. But Shakespeare is beyond
this;—he always by metaphors and figures involves in the
thing considered a universe of past and possible experiences."

(These lines alone should be sufficient answer to those who doubt the authenticity of the scene). When Duncan says, "What he˙ hath lost, Noble *Macbeth* hath wonne," we hear the echo,

> So from that Spring, whence comfort seem'd to come,
>
> Discomfort swells,

—and this is not the only time the Captain's words can be applied in the course of the play. Nor is it fantastic to suppose that in the account of Macdonwald Shakespeare consciously provided a parallel with the Macbeth of the later acts when "The multiplying Villanies of Nature swarme upon him." After all, everybody has noticed the later parallel between Macbeth and Cawdor ("He was a Gentleman, on whom I built an absolute Trust").

A poem works by calling into play, directing and integrating certain interests. If we really accept the suggestion, which then becomes revolutionary, that *Macbeth* is a poem, it is clear that the impulses aroused in Act I, Scenes I and II, are part of the whole response, even if they are not all immediately relevant to the fortunes of the protagonist. If these scenes are "the botching work of an interpolator" he botched to pretty good effect.

In Act I, Scene III, confusion is succeeded by uncertainty. The Witches

> looke not like th' Inhabitants o' th' Earth,
> And yet are on't.

Banquo asks Macbeth,

> Why doe you start, and seeme to feare
> Things that doe sound so faire?

He addresses the Witches,

> You should be women,
> And yet your Beards forbid me to interprete
> That you are so . . . .
> . . . . . i'th' name of truth
> Are ye fantasticall, or that indeed
> Which outwardly ye shew?

When they vanish, "what seem'd corporall" melts "as breath into the Winde." The whole force of the uncertainty of the scene is gathered into Macbeth's soliloquy,

> This supernaturall solliciting
> Cannot be ill; cannot be good . . .

which with its sickening see-saw rhythm completes the impression of "a phantasma, or a hideous dream."[1]   Macbeth's echoing of the

---

[1] The parallel with *Julius Caesar*, Act II, Scene 1, 63–69 is worth notice:

> Between the acting of a dreadfull thing,
> And the first motion, all the Interim is
> Like a Phantasma, or a hideous Dreame . . .

Macbeth speaks of "the Interim," and his "single state of Man" echoes Brutus'

> The state of man,
> Like to a little Kingdome, suffers then
> The nature of an Insurrection.

The rhythm of Macbeth's speech is repeated in Lady Macbeth's

> What thou would'st highly,
> That would'st thou holily, etc.

Witches' "Faire is foule" has often been commented upon.

In contrast to the preceding scenes, Act I, Scene IV suggests the natural order which is shortly to be violated. It stresses: natural relationships—"children," "servants," "sons" and "kinsmen"; honourable bonds and the political order—"liege," "thanes," "service," "duty," "loyalty," "throne," "state" and "honour"; and the human "love" is linked to the more purely natural by images of husbandry. Duncan says to Macbeth,

> I have begun to plant thee, and will labour
> To make thee full of growing.

When he holds Banquo to his heart Banquo replies,

> There if I grow,
> The Harvest is your owne.

Duncan's last speech is worth particular notice,

> . . . in his comméndations, I am fed:
> It is a Banquet to me.

At this point something should be said of what is meant by "the natural order." In *Macbeth* this comprehends both "wild nature"—birds, beasts and reptiles—and humankind since "humane statute purg'd the gentle Weale."

The specifically human aspect is related to the concept of propriety and degree,—

> communities,
> Degrees in Schooles and Brother-hoods in Cities,
> Peacefull Commerce from dividable shores,
> The primogenitive, and due of byrth,
> Prerogative of Age, Crownes, Scepters, Lawrels.

In short, it represents society in harmony with nature, bound by love and friendship, and ordered by law and duty.   It is one of the main axes of reference by which we take our emotional bearings in the play.

In the light of this the scene of Duncan's entry into the castle gains in significance.   The critics have often remarked on the irony.   What is not so frequently observed is that the key words of the scene are "loved," "wooingly," "bed," "procreant Cradle," "breed, and haunt," all images of love and procreation, supernaturally sanctioned, for the associations of "temple-haunting" colour the whole of the speeches of Banquo and Duncan.[1]   We do violence to the play when we ignore Shakespeare's insistence upon the "holy supernatural" as opposed to the "supernaturall solliciting" of the Witches. I shall return to this point.   Meanwhile it is pertinent to remember that Duncan himself is

---

[1] See F. R. Leavis, *How to Teach Reading*, pp. 29–31 for a more detailed analysis of these lines.

"The Lords anoynted Temple" (Act II, Scene
III, 70).[1]

The murder is explicitly presented as unnatural. After the greeting of Ross and Angus,
Macbeth's heart knocks at his ribs "against
the use of Nature." Lady Macbeth fears his
"humane kindnesse"; she wishes herself "un-
sexed," that she may 'be troubled by "no
compunctious visitings of Nature," and invokes
the "murth'ring Ministers" who "wait on
Natures Mischiefe." The murder is committed
when

> Nature seemes dead, and wicked Dreames abuse
> The Curtain'd sleepe,

and it is accompanied by portents "unnaturall,
even like the deed that's done." The sun
remains obscured, and Duncan's horses "Turn'd
wilde in nature." Besides these explicit references to the unnatural we notice the violence
of the imagery—

> I have given Sucke, and know
> How tender 'tis to love the Babe that milkes me,
> I would, while it was smyling in my Face,
> Have pluckt my Nipple from his Bonelesse Gummes,
> And dasht the Braines out. . . .

Not only are the feelings presented unnatural
in this sense, they are also strange—peculiar

[1] Later, Macduff says to Malcolm
> Thy Royall Father
> Was a most Sainted King.
>   (Act IV, Scene III, 108).

compounds which cannot be classified by any
of the usual labels—"fear," "disgust," etc.
Macbeth's words towards the end of Act II,
Scene I serve to illustrate this:—

> Thou sowre [sure] and firme-set Earth
> Heare not my steps, which way they walke, for feare
> Thy very stones prate of my where-about,
> And take the present horror from the time,
> Which now sutes with it.

The first three lines imply a recognition of the
enormity of the crime; Macbeth asks that the
earth ("sure and firme-set" contrasted with the
disembodied "Murder" which "moves like a
Ghost") shall not hear his steps, for if it does
so the very stones will speak and betray him—
thereby breaking the silence and so lessening
the horror. "Take" combines two constructions.
On the one hand, "for fear they take the present
horror from the time" expresses attraction,
identification with the appropriate setting of
his crime. But "take" is also an imperative,
expressing anguish and repulsion. "Which now
sutes with it" implies acceptance, either gloating
or reluctant according to the two meanings of
the previous line. The unusual sliding construction (unusual in ordinary verse, there are
other examples in Shakespeare, and in Donne)
expresses the unusual emotion which is only
crudely analysed if we call it a mixture of
repulsion and attraction fusing into "horror."

"Confusion now hath made his Master-peece,"
and in the lull that follows the discovery of the
murder, Ross and an Old Man as chorus, echo
the theme of unnatural disorder. The scene
(and the act) ends with a "sentence" by the
Old Man which is capable of three interpre-
tations:

Gods benyson go with you, and with those
That would make good of bad, and Friends of Foes.

It may refer to Ross who intends to make the
best of a bad business, by accepting Macbeth
as king.   It may refer to Macduff who is destined
to "make good of bad" by destroying the evil.
More important, in its immediate application
it may refer to Macbeth, for the next movement
is concerned with his attempt to make good of
bad by restoring the natural order; the tragedy
lies in his failure.

A key is found in Macbeth's words spoken
to the men hired to murder Banquo (Act III,
Scene I, 91–100). When Dr. Bradley is discussing the possibility that *Macbeth* has been
abridged he remarks ("very aptly" according to
the Arden editor), "surely, anyone who wanted
to cut the play down would have operated, say,
on Macbeth's talk with Banquo's murderers, or
on Act III, Scene VI, or on the very long dialogue
of Malcolm and Macduff, instead of reducing

D

the most exciting part of the drama."[1] No, the
speech to the murderers is not very "exciting"—
but its function should be obvious to anyone who
is not blinded by Dr. Bradley's preconceptions
about "drama." By accepted canons it is an
irrelevance; actually it stands as a symbol of
the order that Macbeth wishes to restore. In
the catalogue

> Hounds, and Greyhounds, Mungrels, Spaniels, Curres,
> Showghes, Water-Rugs, and Demy-Wolves

are merely "dogs," but Macbeth names each
one individually; and

> the valued file
> Distinguishes the swift, the slow, the subtle,
> The House-keeper, the Hunter, every one
> According to the gift, which bounteous Nature
> Hath in him clos'd.

It is an image of order, each one in his degree.
At the beginning of the scene, we remember,
Macbeth had arranged "a feast," "a solemn
supper," at which "society" should be "welcome." And when alone he suggests the ancient
harmonies by rejecting in idea the symbols of
their contraries—"a fruitlesse Crowne," "a barren
Scepter," and an "unlineall" succession. But

---

[1] *Shakespearean Tragedy*, p. 469. *Macbeth*, Arden
Edition, pp. xxi–xxii. I discuss the importance of Act III,
Scene VI, and of the Malcolm–Macduff dialogue later,
pp. 50–56.

this new "health" is "sickly" whilst Banquo lives, and can only be made "perfect" by his death. In an attempt to recreate an order based on murder, disorder makes fresh inroads. This is made explicit in the next scene (Act III, Scene II). Here the snake, usually represented as the most venomous of creatures, stands for the natural order which Macbeth has "scotched" but which will "close, and be her selfe."[1]

At this point in the play there is a characteristic confusion. At the end of Act III, Scene II, Macbeth says, "Things bad begun, make strong themselves by ill," that is, all that he can do is to ensure his physical security by a second crime, although earlier (Act III, Scene I, 106–107) he had aimed at complete

---

[1] The murder of Banquo, like the murder of Duncan, is presented in its aspect as a violation of natural continuity and natural order. Macbeth will "cancell and teare to pieces that great Bond" which keeps him pale. "Bond" has a more than general significance. The line is clearly associated with Lady Macbeth's "But in them, Natures Coppie's not eterne," and the full force of the words is only brought out if we remember that when Shakespeare wrote them, copyholders formed numerically the largest land-holding class in England whose appeal was always to "immemorial antiquity" and "times beyond the memory of man." The Macbeth–Banquo opposition is emphasized when we learn that Banquo's line will "stretch out to the cracke of Doome" (Act IV, Scene I, 117). Macbeth is cut off from the natural sequence, "He has no children" (Act IV, Scene III, 217), he is a "Monster" (Act V, Scene VII, 54). Macbeth's isolation is fully brought out in the last Act.

"health" by the death of Banquo and Fleance, and later he says that the murder of Fleance would have made him

> perfect,
> Whole as the Marble, founded as the Rocke.
>
> (Act III, Scene iv, 21–22).

The two possibilities are only gradually disentangled.

The situation is magnificently presented in the banquet scene. Here speech, action and symbolism combine. The stage direction *"Banquet prepar'd"* is the first pointer. In Shakespeare, as Mr. Wilson Knight has remarked, banquets are almost invariably symbols of rejoicing, friendship and concord. Significantly, the nobles sit in due order.

Macbeth.	You know your owne degrees, sit downe: At first and last, the hearty welcome.
Lords.	Thankes to your Majesty.
Macbeth.	Our selfe will mingle with Society, And play the humble Host: Our Hostesse keepes her State, but in best time We will require her welcome.
Lady Macbeth.	Pronounce it for me Sir, to all our Friends, For my heart speakes, they are welcome.

Enter first Murderer.

There is no need for comment. In a sense
the scene marks the climax of the play. One
avenue has been explored; "Society," "Host,"
"Hostess," "Friends" and "Welcome" repeat
a theme which henceforward is heard only
faintly until it is taken up in the final orches-
tration, when it appears as "Honor, Love,
Obedience, Troopes of Friends." With the
disappearance of the ghost, Macbeth may be
"a man againe," but he has, irretrievably,

> displac'd the mirth,
> Broke the good meeting, with most admir'd disorder.

The end of the scene is in direct contrast to its
beginning.

> Stand not upon the order of your going,
> But go at once

echoes ironically, "You know your owne degrees,
sit downe."

Before we attempt to disentangle the varied
threads of the last Act, two more scenes call
for particular comment. The first is the scene
in Macduff's castle. Almost without exception
the critics have stressed the pathos of young
Macduff, his "innocent prattle," his likeness to
Arthur, and so on—reactions appropriate to the
work of Sir James Barrie which obscure the

complex dramatic function of the scene.[1]   In
the first place, it echoes in different keys the
theme of the false appearance, of doubt and
confusion.   At its opening we are perplexed
with questions:—Is Macduff a traitor?   If so,
to whom, to Macbeth or to his wife?   Was his
flight due to wisdom or to fear?   Ross says,

> But cruell are the times, when we are Traitors
> And do not know our selves: when we hold Rumor
> From what we feare, yet know not what we feare.

Lady Macduff says of her son,

> Father'd he is,
> And yet hee's Father-lesse.[2]

She teases him with riddles, and he replies with
questions.

Secondly, the scene shows the spreading evil.
As Fletcher has pointed out, Macduff and his
wife are "representatives of the interests of
loyalty and domestic affection."[3]   There is much
more in the death of young Macduff than
"pathos"; the violation of the natural order is

---

[1] Dr. Bradley says of this and the following scene:
"They have a technical value in helping to give the last
stage of the action the form of a conflict between Macbeth
and Macduff.   But their chief function is of another kind.
It is to touch the heart with a sense of beauty and pathos,
to open the springs of love and of tears."—*Shakespearean
Tragedy*, p. 391, see also p. 394.

[2] Compare the equivocation about Macduff's birth.

[3] Quoted by Furness, p. 218.   The whole passage from
Fletcher is worth attention.

completed by the murder. But there is even more than this. That the tide is about to turn against Macbeth is suggested both by the rhythm and imagery of Ross's speech:

> But cruell are the times, when we are Traitors
> And do not know our selves: when we hold Rumor
> From what we feare, yet know not what we feare,
> But floate upon a wilde and violent Sea
> Each way, and move ———[1]

The comma after "way," the complete break after "move," give the rhythm of a tide, pausing at the turn. And when Lady Macduff answers the Murderer's question, "Where is your husband?"

> I hope in no place so unsanctified,
> Where such as thou may'st find him

we recall the associations set up in Act III, Scene VI, a scene of choric commentary upon Macduff's flight to England, to the "pious Edward," "the Holy King."

Although the play moves swiftly, it does not move with a simple directness. Its complex subtleties include cross currents, the ebb and

[1] The substitution of a dash for the full stop after "move" is the only alteration that seems necessary in the Folio text. The other emendations of various editors ruin both the rhythm and the idiom. Ross is in a hurry and breaks off; he begins the next line, "Shall not be long," omitting "I" or "it"—which some editors needlessly restore. In the Folio a colon is used to indicate the breaking off of a sentence in Act V, Scene III, 20.

flow of opposed thoughts and emotions. The scene in Macduff's castle, made up of doubts, riddles, paradoxes and uncertainties, ends with an affirmation, "Thou ly'st thou shagge-ear'd Villaine." But this is immediately followed, not by the downfall of Macbeth, but by a long scene which takes up once more the theme of mistrust, disorder and evil.

The conversation between Macduff and Malcolm has never been adequately explained. We have already seen Dr. Bradley's opinion of it. The Clarendon editors say, "The poet no doubt felt this scene was needed to supplement the meagre parts assigned to Malcolm and Macduff." If this were all, it might be omitted. Actually the Malcolm–Macduff dialogue has at least three functions. Obviously Macduff's audience with Malcolm and the final determination to invade Scotland help on the story, but this is of subordinate importance. It is clear also that Malcolm's suspicion and the long testing of Macduff emphasize the mistrust which has spread from the central evil of the play.[1] But the main purpose of the scene is obscured unless we realize its function as choric commentary.

[1] As an example of the slight strands which are gathered into the pattern of the play consider the function of the third Murderer in Act III, Scene III. It seems that Macbeth has sent him "to make security doubly sure." Only after some doubt do the first two decide that the third "needs not their mistrust."

In alternating speeches the evil which Macbeth
has caused is explicitly stated, without ex-
tenuation. And it is stated impersonally.

> Each new Morne,
> New Widdowes howle, new Orphans cry, new sorowes
> Strike heaven on the face, that it resounds
> As if it felt with Scotland, and yell'd out
> Like Syllable of Dolour.

> Our Country sinkes beneath the yoake,
> It weepes, it bleeds, and each new day a gash
> Is added to her wounds.

> Not in the Legions
> Of horrid Hell, can come a Divell more damn'd
> In evils, to top *Macbeth*

> I grant him Bloody,
> Luxurious, Avaricious, False, Deceitfull,
> Sodaine, Malicious, smacking of every sinne
> That has a name.

With this approach we see the relevance of
Malcolm's self-accusation. He has ceased to be
a person. His lines repeat and magnify the
evils which have already been attributed to
Macbeth, acting as a mirror wherein the ills of
Scotland are reflected. And the statement of
evil is strengthened by contrast with the opposite
virtues, "As Justice, Verity, Temp'rance, Stable-
nesse."

There is no other way in which the scene can

be read.   And if dramatic fitness is not sufficient warrant for this approach, we can refer to the pointers which Shakespeare has provided. Macbeth is "luxurious" and "avaricious," and the first sins mentioned by Malcolm in an expanded statement are lust and avarice.   When he declares,

> Nay, had I powre, I should
> Poure the sweet Milke of Concord, into Hell,
> Uprore the universall peace, confound
> All unity on earth,

we remember that this is what Macbeth has done.[1]   Indeed Macduff is made to answer,

> These Evils thou repeat'st upon thy selfe,
> Hath banish'd me from Scotland.[2]

Up to this point at least the impersonal function of the speaker is predominant.   And even when Malcolm, once more a person in a play, announces

---

[1] For a more specific reference see Act IV, Scene I, 50–61. Macbeth is determined to follow his course even if it causes the worst forms of disorder,

> Though the treasure
> Of Natures Germaine tumble altogether,
> Even till destruction sicken.

[2] "Hath," is third person plural.   See Abbott, *Shakespearian Grammar*, § 334.   I admit the lines are ambiguous but they certainly bear the interpretation I have given them.   Indeed most editors print, "upon thyself Have banished. . . ."

his innocence, it is impossible not to hear the impersonal overtone:

> For even now
> I put my selfe to thy Direction, and
> Unspeake mine owne detraction.   Heere abjure
> The taints, and blames I laide upon my selfe,
> For strangers to my Nature.

He speaks for Scotland, and for the forces of order. The "scotch'd Snake" will "close, and be herselfe."

There are only two alternatives; either Shakespeare was a bad dramatist, or his critics have been badly misled by mistaking the *dramatis personae* for real persons in this scene. Unless of course the ubiquitous Interpolator has been at work upon it.

I have called *Macbeth* a statement of evil; but it is a statement not of a philosophy but of ordered emotion. This ordering is of course a continuous process (hence the importance of the scrupulous analysis of each line), it is not merely something that happens in the last act corresponding to the dénouement or unravelling of the plot. All the same the interests aroused are heightened in the last act before they are finally "placed," and we are given a vantage point from which the whole course of the drama may be surveyed in retrospect. There is no formula which will describe this final effect. It is no use saying that we are "quietened," "purged" or "exalted" at the end of *Macbeth* or of any other tragedy. It is no use taking one step nearer the play and saying we are purged, etc., because we see the downfall of a wicked man or because we realize the justice of Macbeth's doom whilst retaining enough sympathy for him or admiration of his potential qualities to be filled with a sense of "waste." It is no use discussing the effect in abstract terms at all; we can only discuss it in terms of the poet's concrete realization of certain emotions and attitudes.

At this point it is necessary to return to what I have already said (p. 40) about the importance of images of grace and of the holy supernatural in the play. In his essay on Dante, Mr. Eliot remarks, "It is apparently easier to accept damnation as poetic material than purgation or beatitude; less is involved that is strange to the modern mind."[1] It is perhaps because the idea of beatitude is strange to the modern mind that for the last hundred years or so the critics have not only sentimentalized Macbeth—ignoring the completeness with which Shakespeare shows his final identification with evil—but they have slurred the passages in which the positive good

[1] *Dante*, p. 36 (*Selected Essays*, p. 239).

is presented by means of religious symbols. In Act III the banquet scene is immediately[1] followed by a scene in which Lennox and another Lord (both completely impersonal) discuss the situation; the last half of their dialogue is of particular importance. The verse has none of the power of, say, Macbeth's soliloquies, but it would be a mistake to call it undistinguished; it is serenely harmonious, and its tranquillity contrasts with the turbulence of the scenes which immediately precede it and follow it, as its images of grace contrast with their "toile and trouble." Macduff has fled to "the Pious Edward," "the Holy King," who has received Malcolm "with such grace." Lennox prays for the aid of "some holy Angell,"

> that a swift blessing
> May soone returne to this our suffering Country,
> Under a hand accurs'd.

[1] If we omit Act III, Scene v where for once the editors' "spurious" may be allowed to stand. I thought at first that Shakespeare intended to portray the Witches at this point as rather shoddy creatures, thereby intensifying the general irony. Certainly the rhythm of Hecate's speech is banal—but so is the obvious rhythm of *Sweeney Agonistes*, and it does provide a contrast with the harmony of the verse in the next scene. Certainly also Shakespeare did not intend to portray the Witches as in any way "dignified" ("Dignified, impressive, sexless beings, ministers of fate and the supernatural powers . . . existing in the elemental poetry of wind and storm"—*Macbeth*, Arden Edition, p. xlii). But the verse is too crude to serve even this purpose.

And the "other Lord" answers, "Ile send my
Prayers with him." Many of the phrases are
general and abstract—"grace," "the malevolence
of Fortune," "his high respect"—but one passage
has an individual particularity that gives it
prominence:

> That by the helpe of these (with him above
> To ratifie the Worke) we may againe
> Give to our Tables meate, sleepe to our Nights:
> Free from our Feasts, and Banquets bloody knives;
> Do faithful Homage, and receive free Honors,
> All which we pine for now.

Food and sleep, society and the political order
are here, as before, represented as supernaturally
sanctioned. I have suggested that this passage
is recalled for a moment in Lady Macduff's
answer to the Murderer (Act IV, Scene II, 80),
and it is certainly this theme which is taken up
when the Doctor enters in Act IV, Scene III;
the reference to the King's Evil may be a compli-
ment to King James, but it is not merely that.
We have only to remember that the unseen
Edward stands for the powers that are to prove
"the Med'cine of the sickly Weale" of Scotland
to see the double meaning in

> there are a crew of wretched Soules
> That stay his Cure . . . .

Their disease "is called the Evill." The
"myraculous worke," the "holy Prayers," "the

healing Benediction," Edward's "vertue," the
"sundry Blessings . . . that speake him full
of Grace" are reminders not only of the evil
against which Malcolm is seeking support,
but of the positive qualities against which
the evil and disorder must be measured. Scat-
tered notes ("Gracious England," "Christen-
dome," "heaven," "gentle Heavens") remind us
of the theme until the end of the scene when we
know that Macbeth (the "Hell-Kite," "this
Fiend of Scotland")

> Is ripe for shaking, and the Powers above
> Put on their Instruments.

The words quoted are not mere formalities;
they have a positive function, and help to determine the way in which we shall respond to the
final scenes.

The description of the King's Evil (Act IV,
Scene III, 141–159) has a particular relevance;
it is directly connected with the disease metaphors
of the last Act[1]; and these are strengthened by
combining within themselves the ideas of disorder and of the unnatural which run throughout

---

[1] The original audience would be helped to make the
connexion if, as is likely, the Doctor of Act IV, Scene III,
and the Doctor of Act V were played by the same actor,
probably without any change of dress. We are not meant
to think of two Doctors in the play (Dr. A of Harley
Street and Dr. B of Edinburgh) but simply, in each case,
of "a Doctor."

the play. Lady Macbeth's sleepwalking is a "slumbry agitation," and "a great perturbation in Nature." Some say Macbeth is "mad." We hear of his "distemper'd cause," and of his "pester'd senses" which

> recoyle and start,
> When all that is within him, do's condemne
> It selfe, for being there.

In the play general impressions are pointed by reference to the individual and particular (cf. Act IV, Scene III, where "the general cause" is given precision by the "Fee-griefe due to some single breast"); whilst at the same time particular impressions are reflected and magnified. Not only Macbeth and his wife but the whole land is sick. Caithness says,

> Meet we the Med'cine of the sickly Weale,
> And with him poure we in our Countries purge,
> Each drop of us.

And Lennox replies,

> Or so much as it needes,
> To dew the Soveraigne Flower, and drowne the Weeds
> (Act V, Scene II, 27–30).

—an admirable example, by the way, of the kind of fusion already referred to, since we have not only the weed-flower opposition, but a continuation of the medical metaphor in "Soveraigne," which means both "royal" and "powerfully remedial."[1] And the images of health and disease are clearly related to moral good and evil. The Doctor says of Lady Macbeth,

> More needs she the Divine, than the Physitian:
> God, God forgive us all.

Macbeth asks him,

> Can'st thou not Minister to a minde diseas'd,
> Plucke from the Memory a rooted Sorrow,
> Raze out the written troubles of the Braine,
> And with some sweet Oblivious Antidote
> Cleanse the stufft bosome, of that perillous stuffe
> Which weighes upon the heart?

There is terrible irony in his reply to the Doctor's "Therein the Patient must minister to himselfe": "Throw Physicke to the Dogs, Ile none of it."

We have already noticed the association of the ideas of disease and of the unnatural in these final scenes—

> unnatural deeds
> Do breed unnatural troubles,

---

[1] Macbeth himself says,
> If thou could'st Doctor, cast
> The Water of my Land, finde her Disease,
> And purge it to a sound and pristine Health,
> I would applaud thee to the very Eccho.
And he continues,
> What Rubarb, Senna, or what Purgative drugge
> Would scowre these English hence?
>   (Act V, Scene III, 50–56).
The characteristic reversal (the English forces represented as an impurity which has to be "scoured") need not surprise us.

and there is propriety in Macbeth's highly
charged metaphor,

> My way of life
> Is falne into the Seare, the yellow Leafe.

But the unnatural has now another part to play,
in the peculiar "reversal" that takes place at
the end of *Macbeth*. Hitherto the agent of
the unnatural has been Macbeth. Now it is
Malcolm who commands Birnam Wood to
move, it is "the good Macduff" who reveals
his unnatural birth, and the opponents of
Macbeth whose "deere causes" would "excite
the mortified man." Hitherto Macbeth has
been the deceiver, "mocking the time with
fairest show"; now Malcolm orders,

> Let every Souldier hew him downe a Bough,
> And bear't before him, thereby shall we shadow
> The numbers of our Hoast, and make discovery
> Erre in report of us.

Our first reaction is to make some such remark
as "Nature becomes unnatural in order to rid
itself of Macbeth." But this is clearly inade-
quate; we have to translate it and define our
impressions in terms of our response to the
play at this point. By associating with the
opponents of evil the ideas of deceit and of the
unnatural, previously associated solely with Macbeth and the embodiments of evil, Shakespeare
emphasizes the disorder and at the same time
frees our minds from the burden of the horror.

After all, the movement of Birnam Wood and Macduff's unnatural birth have a simple enough explanation.

There is a parallel here with the disorder of the last Act. It begins with Lady Macbeth sleepwalking—a "slumbry agitation"—and the remaining scenes are concerned with marches, stratagems, fighting, suicide, and death in battle. If we merely read the play we are liable to overlook the importance of the sights and sounds which are obvious on the stage. The frequent stage directions should be observed—*Drum and Colours, Enter Malcolm . . . and Soldiers Marching, A Cry within of Women*—and there are continuous directions for *Alarums, Flourishes*, and fighting. Macduff orders,

> Make all our Trumpets speak, give them all breath,
> Those clamorous Harbingers of Blood, and Death,

and he traces Macbeth by the noise of fighting:

> That way the noise is: Tyrant shew thy face.
>   . . . There thou should'st be,
> By this great clatter, one of greatest note
> Seemes bruited.

There are other suggestions of disorder throughout the Act. Macbeth

> cannot buckle his distemper'd cause
> Within the belt of Rule.

He orders, "Come, put mine Armour on," and almost in the same breath, "Pull't off I say."

His "Royal Preparation" is a noisy confusion. He wishes "th' estate o' th' world were now undon," though the tone is changed now since he bade the Witches answer him,

> Though bladed Corne be lodg'd, and Trees blown
> downe,
> Though Castles topple on their Warders heads:
> Though Pallaces, and Pyramids do slope
> Their heads to their Foundations.

But all this disorder has now a positive tendency, towards the good which Macbeth had attempted to destroy, and which he names as "Honor, Love, Obedience, Troopes of Friends." At the beginning of the battle Malcolm says,

> Cosins, I hope the dayes are neere at hand
> That Chambers will be safe,

and Menteith answers, "We doubt it nothing." Siward takes up the theme of certainty as opposed to doubt:

> Thoughts speculative, their unsure hopes relate,
> But certaine issue, stroakes must arbitrate,
> Towards which, advance the warre.

And doubt and illusion are finally dispelled:

> Now neere enough:
> Your leavy Skreenes throw downe,
> And shew like those you are.

By now there should be no danger of our misinterpreting the greatest of Macbeth's final speeches.

Life's but a walking Shadow, a poore Player,
That struts and frets his houre upon the Stage,
And then is heard no more. It is a Tale
Told by an Ideot, full of sound and fury
Signifying nothing.

The theme of the false appearance is revived—
with a difference. It is not only that Macbeth
sees life as deceitful, but the poetry is so fine
that we are almost bullied into accepting an
essential ambiguity in the final statement of the
play, as though Shakespeare were expressing his
own "philosophy" in the lines. But the speech is
"placed" by the tendency of the last Act[1] (order
emerging from disorder, truth emerging from
behind deceit), culminating in the recognition of
the Witches' equivocation ("And be these Jugling
Fiends no more believ'd . . . "), the death of
Macbeth, and the last words of Siward, Macduff
and Malcolm (Act V, Scene VII, 64–105).

This tendency has behind it the whole weight
of the positive values which Shakespeare has
already established, and which are evoked in
Macbeth's speech—

My way of life
Is falne into the Seare, the yellow Leafe,
And that which should accompany Old-Age,
As Honor, Love, Obedience, Troopes of Friends,
I must not looke to have: but in their stead,
Curses, not lowd but deepe, Mouth-honor, breath
Which the poore heart would faine deny, and dare not.

---

[1] Contrast the effect of the last words of Mr. Kurtz in
Heart of Darkness.

Dr. Bradley claims, on the strength of this and the "To-morrow, and to-morrow" speech, that Macbeth's "ruin is never complete.   To the end he never totally loses our sympathy . . . .   In the very depths a gleam of his native love of goodness, and with it a tinge of tragic grandeur, rests upon him." Dr. Bradley's emotion is out of place; the statement is impersonal. It is the keystone of the system which gives emotional coherence to the play. Certainly the system will remain obscured if we concentrate our attention upon "the two great terrible figures, who dwarf all the remaining characters of the drama," if we ignore the "unexciting" or "undramatic scenes," or if conventional "sympathy for the hero" is allowed to distort the pattern of the whole.

I must repeat that I have no illusions about the adequacy of these remarks as criticism; they are merely pointers.[1] But if we follow them our criticism at least will not be deflected, by too great a stress upon "personality," into inquiries into "latent motives and policies not avowed," or into pseudo-critical investigations which are only slightly parodied by the title of this essay.

[1] See Note B.

NOTES

A. (See p. 23).

William Richardson illustrates so well the main tendencies of later eighteenth century criticism that a few quotations seem permissible. (The page references are to the fifth edition, 1797, of the *Essays on Some of Shakespeare's Dramatic Characters* which incorporated his Essays "On Shakespeare's Imitation of Female Characters" and "On the Faults of Shakespeare"):—

" 'The operations of the mind,' as has been well observed by an anonymous writer . . . 'are more complex than those of the body: its motions are progressive: its transitions abrupt and instantaneous: its attitude uncertain and momentary . . . . It would therefore be of great importance to philosophical scrutiny, if the position of the mind, in any given circumstances, could be fixed till it was deliberately surveyed: if the causes which alter its feelings and operations could be accurately shewn, and their effects ascertained with precision.' To accomplish these ends, the dramatic writers, and particularly Shakespeare, may be of the greatest use. An attempt has accordingly been made . . . to employ the light which he affords us in illustrating some curious and interesting views of human nature.

"In Macbeth, misled by an overgrown and gradually perverted passion, 'we trace the progress of that corruption, by which the virtues of the mind are made to contribute to the completion of its depravity' [He is quoting Burke]. In Hamlet we have a striking representation of the pain, of the dejection, and contention of spirit, produced in a person, not only of exquisite, but of moral, and correct sensibility, by the conviction of extreme enormity of conduct in those whom he loves, or wishes to love . . . . King Lear illustrates, that mere sensibility, uninfluenced by a sense of propriety, leads men to an extravagant expression both of social and unsocial feelings," and so on (pp. 395–397).

"In the faithful display of character, he has not hitherto been surpassed . . . . If we consider the sentiments and actions, attributed by the poet to his various characters, as so many facts; if we observe their agreement or disagreement, their aim or their origin; and if we class them according to their common qualities . . . we shall ascertain with some accuracy, the truth of the representation . . . . Thus the moralist becomes a critic: and the two sciences of ethics and criticism appear to be intimately and very naturally connected." (pp. 398–399.)

The essay on the Character of Macbeth ends: "Thus, by considering the rise and progress of a ruling passion, and the fatal consequences of its indulgence, we have shown how a beneficent mind may become inhuman: and how those who are naturally of an amiable temper, if they suffer themselves to be corrupted, will become more ferocious and more unhappy than men of a constitution originally hard and unfeeling. The formation of our characters depends considerably upon ourselves; for we may improve or vitiate every principle we receive from nature" (p. 68). Shakespeare indeed "furnishes excellent illustrations of many passions and affections, and of many singular combinations of passion, affection and ability," (p. 397).

Mrs. Montagu places character delineation among "the chief purposes of theatrical representation" (*An Essay on the Writings and Genius of Shakespeare*, fifth edition, 1785, pp. 19–20), and speaks of Shakespeare's "invariable attention to consistency of character."

On "The Appreciation of Characters" and "The Psychologizing of Shakespeare" in the later eighteenth century, see Chapters XI and XII of R. W. Babcock's *The Genesis of Shakespeare Idolatry, 1766–1799*, from which I extract some further illuminating quotations:

"We always behold the portrait of living nature [in Shakespeare] and find ourselves surrounded with our fellows"—*The Lady's Magazine*, 1784.

"Shakespeare's characters have that appearance of reality which always has the effect of actual life."—William Jackson, *Thirty Letters*, 1782.

". . . the historical dramas of Shakespeare. The wonder-working power of the poet's pen is there most eminently displayed . . . . His characters . . . are such genuine copies from life, that we must suppose the originals acted and spoke in the manner he represents them."—Richard Hole ["T.O."] in the Exeter Society *Essays*, 1796.

Shakespeare's characters "are masterly copies from nature; differing each from the other, and animated as the originals though correct to a scrupulous precision."—T. Whately, *Remarks on Some of the Characters of Shakespeare*, 1785.

I should like to acknowledge my indebtedness to Mr. Babcock's extremely thorough piece of research.

B.   (See p. 64).

A note on some of the books referred to on p. 1 may supply the deficiencies: few of them are by professed Shakespeare critics. *Seven Types of Ambiguity* by W. Empson (Chatto and Windus) contains some admirable examples of the kind of analysis referred to on p. 31, though to say merely this is hardly to do it justice.

The chapter on Hopkins in *New Bearings in*

English Poetry by F. R. Leavis (Chatto and Windus) has helped me, at least, to read Shakespeare more effectively. ("Hopkins' imagery, and his way of using the body and movement of the language are like Shakespeare's.") And I may refer to the same writer's *How to Teach Reading* (published uniform with this essay) which has a direct bearing upon the reading of Shakespeare. Mr. T. S. Eliot's essay on "The Metaphysical Poets" is a necessary part of any "Prelude to Shakespeare," and his essays on Shakespeare and other Elizabethan dramatists (see his *Selected Essays*, Faber and Faber) are not only important in themselves, they suggest for the benefit of others the profitable approach which is the antithesis of that described in Part I of this essay.

Elizabethan Stage Conditions, A Study of Their Place in the Interpretation of Shakespeare's Plays by M. C. Bradbrook (Cambridge University Press) does much to dissolve current misconceptions. *Leading Motives in the Imagery of Shakespeare's Tragedies* by Miss Caroline Spurgeon is useful for those who know how to use it. (It is a pity that Miss Spurgeon emphasizes that she has "listed and classified and card indexed and counted every image in every play thrice over." Those who imagine that a card index is a substitute for sensibility need no encouraging.)

Of the books of "pure" Shakespeare criticism

that have appeared of recent years I consider *The Wheel of Fire* and *The Imperial Theme* by G. Wilson Knight (Oxford) to be the most important. Since writing my essay I have been embarrassed to find how much of my criticism of *Macbeth* is directly indebted to the admirable essay on *The Life Themes in Macbeth* in *The Imperial Theme.* I have decided to let the *Macbeth* pages stand as written, however, since to prune away all that clearly derives from Mr. Knight would be to distort the portions that I consider original, and which I need to support my thesis.

Admiration for Mr. Knight's work must be tempered with reservations.[1] A preoccupation with imagery and symbols, unless minutely controlled by a sensitive intelligence directed upon the text, leads to abstractions almost as dangerous as does a preoccupation with "character." For instance, it is no use thinking we have done anything very important when we have collected all the erotic images (or images of disorder, etc.) in a play; everything depends upon how they are used in a precise particular context. There are passages in *The Imperial Theme* that serve as a warning. I hope this does not seem ungracious; the warning applies equally to my own attempt at elucidation.

[1] I have recorded both my admiration and some of my reservations in a review of *The Imperial Theme—The Criterion*, April, 1932, pp. 540–543.